THE POWER OF CONNECTION:

Understanding Why the World Needs It

By

Chasity Bailey, M.A, J.D.

and

Tomos Archer

INTRODUCTION

WHY ITS IMPORTANT

In an increasingly disconnected world, the need for connection has never been greater due to several factors that have emerged in recent times.

Technological advancements: While technology has undoubtedly made our lives more convenient, it has also created a paradoxical effect of increased isolation. Social media, for instance, can create a false sense of connection without the depth and authenticity that face-to-face interactions provide. This virtual connection often replaces genuine human connection, leading to feelings of loneliness and disconnection.

Individualism and societal changes: Our modern society has become more individualistic, with a shift towards prioritizing personal achievements, career success, and self-interest. This focus on individualism can lead to a neglect of forming and nurturing meaningful connections. As people become consumed with their own pursuits, they often miss out on the benefits that connection with others can bring, such as emotional support, shared experiences, and a sense of belonging.

Globalization and cultural diversity: Globalization has brought people from different cultures, backgrounds, and beliefs closer together. While this can be a tremendous opportunity for growth and understanding, it can also create a sense of divisiveness and misunderstanding. Connection becomes essential in this context to bridge the gaps between cultures, foster empathy, and promote mutual respect and collaboration.

Mental and emotional well-being: Numerous studies have shown the psychological and emotional benefits of connection. People who have strong social connections tend to have better mental health, experience lower rates of depression and anxiety, and have a higher overall sense of well-being. In an era where mental health is increasingly recognized as a crucial aspect of individual and societal health, connection becomes vital in promoting emotional resilience and combating the negative psychological effects of isolation.

Tackling big global challenges: The world is facing significant challenges, such as climate change, poverty, inequality, and political unrest. These issues cannot be effectively addressed without connection and collaboration on a global scale. By fostering connections between individuals, communities, and nations, we can pool our resources, knowledge, and skills to find innovative solutions and build a more sustainable and equitable future.

Ultimately, in an increasingly disconnected world, the need for human connection has never been greater.

Connection is not only a basic human need but also a powerful means for personal growth, societal progress, and global unity. It is through genuine connections that we find support, understanding, and inspiration, and it is through these connections that we can work together to create a more compassionate, empathetic, and interconnected world.

THE SIGNIFICANCE OF CONNECTION

Connection holds immense significance as it affects individuals, communities, and the world in profound ways. Here are some key points to consider:

Impact on Individuals: Connection plays a pivotal role in our personal lives, influencing our overall well-being and happiness. Meaningful connections provide a sense of belonging, emotional support, and validation, which contribute to improved mental and emotional health. It fosters personal growth, as interactions with others offer opportunities for learning, expanding perspectives, and gaining valuable insights. Additionally, strong connections can boost self-esteem, decrease feelings of loneliness and isolation, and enhance overall life satisfaction.

Influence on Communities: Connection is the backbone of flourishing communities. When individuals within a community are connected, social bonds strengthen, leading to increased trust, cooperation, and solidarity. Connected communities thrive as they foster positive social interactions, encourage collaboration, and support collective well-being. Vibrant communities that prioritize connection tend to experience reduced crime rates, improved educational outcomes, and enhanced overall quality of life for their members.

Contribution to the World: In today's interconnected global society, connection is crucial for addressing pressing global challenges. In an increasingly complex world, no single individual or nation can tackle these challenges alone. With strong connections built on respect, empathy, and shared understanding, people can form synergistic partnerships to create a collective impact. Collaboration between individuals, communities, and countries enables the pooling of resources, knowledge, and expertise to address issues like poverty, climate change, inequality, and political conflicts effectively.

Promotion of Empathy and Understanding: Connection nurtures empathy, the ability to understand and share the feelings of others. By connecting with diverse individuals and communities, we develop a broader understanding of different perspectives, cultures, and lived experiences. This empathy helps dismantle stereotypes, biases, and discrimination, fostering a more inclusive and tolerant world. Connection leads to dialogue, open-mindedness, and a willingness to bridge divides, promoting harmony and peaceful coexistence.

Source of Inspiration and Innovation: Connected individuals and communities serve as a source of inspiration and innovation. Shared goals, passions, and knowledge create fertile ground for creative problem-solving and generating groundbreaking ideas. Collaboration and connection facilitate the exchange of ideas and expertise, leading to innovative solutions that address complex societal challenges.

In summary, connection holds immense significance for individuals seeking personal growth, communities striving for prosperity, and our world aiming for unity and progress. It forms the foundation for empathy, understanding, and collaborative endeavor, ensuring that we can build a brighter future together. By recognizing and nurturing the power of connection, we can positively transform ourselves, our communities, and the world at large.

OVERVIEW:

The purpose of this book is to comprehensively explore the multiple facets of connection and shed light on its critical role in fostering meaningful relationships, personal growth, societal progress, and global unity. Throughout the chapters, readers will delve into the various dimensions of connection and gain a deeper understanding of its profound impact on different aspects of life.

By presenting compelling research, real-life stories, and thought-provoking insights, this book aims to demonstrate the significance of connection in our increasingly disconnected world. It underscores the importance of establishing and nurturing genuine connections in order to lead fulfilling lives, build stronger communities, and contribute to positive global transformations.

Through an engaging exploration of the topic, readers will:

Understand the fundamental human need for connection and its impact on overall well-being.

Gain insights into how connection enables the development of meaningful and fulfilling relationships, both personally and interpersonally.

Discover how connection contributes to personal growth, fostering resilience, empathy, and self-discovery.

Explore how connection in communities promotes social cohesion, cooperation, and collective progress.

Reflect on the potential of connection to drive societal advancements, break down barriers, and tackle global challenges.

Envision a more connected and inclusive world, where unity, understanding, and collaboration prevail.

By illuminating the multifaceted nature of connection and highlighting its significance across personal, communal, and global levels, this book aims to inspire readers to prioritize connection in their lives. It encourages readers to forge meaningful relationships, cultivate empathy, and actively contribute to creating a more interconnected and compassionate world.

Ultimately, the book asserts that connection is not only a basic human need but also a transformative force capable of shaping our individual experiences, strengthening our communities, and fostering unity and progress on a global scale.

CHAPTER 1: THE HUMAN NEED FOR CONNECTION

THE FUNDAMENTAL NEED FOR CONNECTION

The fundamental need for connection is deeply rooted in human biology and psychology, reflecting our evolutionary history and shaping our emotional well-being.

From a biological perspective, humans are social beings. Our brains are wired to seek and form connections with others. Research has shown that various neural systems and hormones, such as oxytocin and dopamine, play a significant role in facilitating social bonding. These biological mechanisms reinforce the importance of connection for our survival and reproduction.

Psychologically, connection fulfills our basic psychological needs. Psychologist Abraham Maslow's famous hierarchy of needs includes a sense of belongingness and love as one of the fundamental human needs. According to Maslow, after fulfilling physiological needs like food and shelter, humans strive to fulfill their need for connection and love. Connection provides us with a sense of identity, acceptance, and emotional support that contribute to our psychological well-being.

Moreover, attachment theory, developed by psychologist John Bowlby, emphasizes the importance of early social connections. It highlights the significance of secure attachment bonds between infants and their caregivers for healthy emotional development. These early connections serve as a foundation for establishing relationships throughout our lives.

The absence or deprivation of connection can have profound negative effects on our biology and psychology. Studies have shown that social isolation and loneliness can lead to increased levels of stress hormones, weakened immune system functioning, and higher risks of mental health issues such as depression and anxiety. In severe cases, chronic social isolation may even lead to a shorter lifespan.

On the other hand, meaningful connections offer numerous benefits for our emotional well-being. Sharing experiences, emotions, and support with others helps regulate stress, boosts self-esteem, and enhances overall life satisfaction. Furthermore, positive relationships provide a sense of purpose, meaning, and belonging, which are essential for our psychological fulfillment.

In summary, the fundamental need for connection is deeply rooted in our biology and psychology. It is a basic human need that is necessary for our survival, emotional well-being, and overall functioning. Recognizing and embracing this need for connection can have significant positive impacts on our physical and mental health, as well as our sense of fulfillment and happiness.

THE EVOLUTIONARY PERSPECTIVE

The evolutionary perspective suggests that humans have always sought and benefited from connection due to its crucial role in our survival and reproductive success as a species.

Throughout human history, our ancestors lived in small social groups where cooperation and connection were essential for survival. In these groups, individuals relied on each other for protection from predators, gathering food, and sharing resources. Being socially connected increased the chances of survival and reproduction by promoting collective defense, hunting, and child-rearing.

The evolutionary need for connection is evident in the development of our brain and social behavior. Our brain has evolved specific neural circuits dedicated to social processing, such as the mirror neuron system, which enables us to understand and imitate the actions and emotions of others. This capacity is crucial for communication, empathy, and building social connections.

Moreover, human evolution has favored the development of altruistic behaviors, such as cooperation and empathy, which strengthen social bonds. Acts of kindness and support within social groups increase the overall well-being of individuals and enhance the group's collective success. From an evolutionary perspective, such altruistic behavior is beneficial because it promotes reciprocity and cooperative interactions, fostering the survival and success of the group as a whole.

In addition to promoting survival, connection has played a crucial role in human reproduction. Pair bonding and forming long-term relationships have been vital for raising offspring, maximizing their chances of survival, and ensuring the continuation of genes. Creating strong emotional bonds with a partner and caring for offspring together has provided a significant evolutionary advantage.

The evolutionary perspective also explains our innate desire for social acceptance and belonging. In our ancestral environments, being ostracized from the group could lead to isolation, increased vulnerability, and diminished chances of survival. Seeking connection and acceptance ensured our inclusion and the benefits that come with being part of a supportive social network.

In modern times, although social dynamics have changed, our evolutionary need for connection remains the same. We still seek connection because it fulfills our primal instinct for social bonding, cooperation, and support. The benefits of connection extend beyond survival to encompass emotional well-being, mental health, and a sense of purpose and fulfillment.

In summary, throughout human evolution, connection has been essential for survival, reproductive success, and overall well-being. From our brain's structure to our innate social behaviors, humans have always sought and benefited from connection. Recognizing and nurturing these evolutionary drives can lead to happier, healthier, and more fulfilling lives.

THE CONSEQUENCES OF DEPRIVATION AND ISOLATION

Deprivation and isolation can have significant negative consequences on both mental and physical health. Here are some key consequences associated with the lack of connection:

Mental Health Impact:

Increased risk of depression and anxiety: Lack of social connection has been associated with higher rates of depression and anxiety disorders. The absence of supportive relationships and emotional bonds can lead to feelings of loneliness, hopelessness, and decreased psychological well-being.

Impaired cognitive functioning: Isolation and deprivation of social interaction have been linked to reduced cognitive abilities, including memory decline, decreased attention span, and impaired problem-solving skills.

Higher likelihood of substance abuse: Individuals without strong social connections may be more susceptible to engaging in substance abuse as a means to cope with loneliness and emotional distress.

Physical Health Impact:

Weakened immune system: Isolation and lack of social

connection have been associated with weakened immune system functioning. Chronic social isolation can increase the levels of stress hormones and inflammation in the body, making individuals more susceptible to illnesses and diseases.

Higher risk of cardiovascular problems: Research indicates that socially isolated individuals are at a higher risk of developing cardiovascular diseases, including heart attacks and strokes. Social support and connection have a protective effect on cardiovascular health.

Increased mortality risk: Prolonged social isolation and loneliness have been associated with higher mortality rates. The lack of connection can contribute to various health problems, including chronic diseases, mental health disorders, and reduced life expectancy.

Emotional Well-being:

Decreased subjective well-being: A lack of connection can lead to decreased overall life satisfaction and subjective well-being. The absence of positive social interactions and emotional support can contribute to a sense of emptiness and dissatisfaction.

Overall, deprivation and isolation have significant consequences for both mental and physical health. Connection and social support play a vital role in promoting psychological well-being, maintaining physical health, and increasing resilience in the face of stressors. It highlights the importance of nurturing and prioritizing meaningful relationships and social connections to safeguard our mental and physical well-being.

CHAPTER 2: CONNECTION AND PERSONAL RELATIONSHIPS

THE ROLE OF CONNECTION IN MAINTAINING RELATIONSHIPS.

Connection plays a pivotal role in forming and maintaining healthy relationships. It provides the foundation for emotional intimacy, trust, and mutual understanding. Here are some key aspects that highlight the significance of connection in relationships:

Building Emotional Intimacy: Connection fosters emotional intimacy, which involves deep emotional closeness, vulnerability, and trust between individuals. Through open and honest communication, active listening, and empathy, connection allows partners to share their thoughts, feelings, and desires without judgment. This emotional intimacy creates a strong bond and a sense of security within the relationship.

Strengthening Trust and Security: Connection is essential for building and maintaining trust within relationships. Through consistent emotional support and understanding, partners feel safe to share their vulnerabilities and rely on each other in times of need. Trust grows through shared experiences, shared values, and a strong sense of connection built on open and transparent communication.

Enhancing Communication: Connection paves the way for effective communication in relationships. When individuals feel connected, they are more likely to express themselves honestly and respectfully, listen attentively, and seek mutual understanding. This open and empathetic communication fosters a deeper connection and helps address conflicts or concerns constructively.

Promoting Relationship Satisfaction: Connection is vital for overall relationship satisfaction. Feeling emotionally connected to a partner increases feelings of happiness, contentment, and fulfillment within the relationship. Sharing experiences, creating shared memories, and enjoying meaningful activities together strengthen the bond between partners and contribute to long-term relationship satisfaction.

Supporting Empathy and Understanding: Connection promotes empathy and understanding between partners. When individuals feel connected, they are more likely to empathize with their partner's emotions, perspectives, and needs. This understanding helps build a strong foundation of mutual support, validation, and compassion within the relationship.

Nurturing Growth and Adaptation: Connection is crucial for personal growth and the growth of the relationship. Through connection, partners support each other's individual development, encourage each other's goals, and help each other overcome challenges. A strong connection enables partners to adapt and grow together as they face the inevitable ups and downs of life.

In summary, connection forms the core of healthy relationships. It builds emotional intimacy, trust, and effective communication. It creates a safe and supportive space for partners to share their vulnerabilities and experiences. Moreover, connection fosters empathy, understanding, and personal growth within the relationship. By prioritizing and nurturing connection, couples can cultivate and maintain thriving, healthy relationships.

DISCUSS THE DIFFERENT FORMS OF CONNECTION

Connection can take various forms, each offering unique dimensions of intimacy and fulfillment within relationships. Here are different forms of connection and their impact:

Emotional Connection: Emotional connection involves a deep understanding and empathetic bond between individuals. It is rooted in sharing emotions, experiences, and vulnerabilities, allowing partners to feel seen, heard, and emotionally supported. Emotional connection fosters intimacy and trust, providing a sense of security and belonging in the relationship. It contributes to a fulfilling partnership characterized by emotional closeness and mutual support.

Intellectual Connection: Intellectual connection is based on shared interests, stimulating conversations, and a mutual appreciation for each other's intellectual pursuits. This form of connection involves engaging in discussions, exchanging ideas, and challenging each other intellectually. Intellectual connection fuels mental stimulation and growth, fostering a sense of intellectual intimacy and mutual respect within the relationship.

Spiritual Connection: Spiritual connection goes beyond religious beliefs and is centered around shared values, purpose, and philosophical perspectives. When partners share a spiritual connection, they support each other's spiritual growth and engage in meaningful discussions about life's purpose and values. This connection helps deepen understanding and provides a sense of meaning, fulfillment, and shared purpose in the relationship.

Physical and Sexual Connection: Physical and sexual connection involves intimacy, affection, and sexual compatibility. It includes both emotional and physical components, encompassing physical touch, sexual desire, and a deep physical bond between partners. This form of connection contributes to physical and emotional well-being, enhances relationship satisfaction, and fosters a sense of physical and sexual fulfillment.

Social Connection: Social connection focuses on the shared social networks, friendships, and social activities within a partnership. Couples who have a strong social connection actively participate in social engagements together, have shared friendships, and support each other's social needs. Social connection brings a sense of belonging within a broader community and enhances the overall enjoyment and sense of fulfillment in the relationship.

The impact of these different forms of connection on intimacy and fulfillment may vary from couple to couple based on individual preferences and relationship dynamics. However, cultivating a balance of multiple forms of connection is typically associated with greater satisfaction, depth, and long-term fulfillment in relationships. It is important for partners to actively nurture and prioritize these different forms of connection in order to create a well-rounded and deeply fulfilling partnership.

COMMON CHALLENGES IN MAINTAINING CONNECTIONS.

Maintaining connections in the face of challenges posed by technology, busy lifestyles, and societal pressures can be demanding, but not impossible. Here are some common challenges and strategies to overcome them:

Technology and Distraction:

- Challenge: Technology, while offering various communication tools, can also contribute to distraction and superficial connection. Excessive reliance on technology can hinder genuine, meaningful connections.

- Strategy: Establish boundaries with technology, such as designated device-free times or areas, to ensure uninterrupted quality time for connection. Practice active listening and be fully present during conversations. Make an effort to prioritize face-to-face interactions whenever possible, as they promote deeper connections.

Busy Lifestyles:

- Challenge: Busy lifestyles with demanding work schedules, family commitments, and personal responsibilities leave little time for connection with loved ones.

- Strategy: Prioritize quality over quantity. Dedicate focused and intentional time for connection by scheduling regular date nights, family outings, or dedicated moments for meaningful conversations. Look for opportunities to integrate connection into daily routines, such as preparing meals together or taking walks as a means to reconnect.

Societal Pressures:

- Challenge: Societal pressures, including societal norms, cultural expectations, or external judgment, can strain connections by creating barriers or causing conflicts.

- Strategy: Foster open and honest communication within relationships to navigate societal pressures constructively. Establish a safe space to express individual needs, aspirations, and concerns without fear of judgment. Focus on shared values and beliefs to build a strong foundation. Surround yourself with a supportive network that encourages authentic connections and respects individual choices.

Communication Challenges:

- Challenge: Miscommunication or lack of effective communication can hinder connection, leading to misunderstandings and conflict.

- Strategy: Practice active listening and empathy in communication. Strive for clarity, share openly, and encourage partners to express their thoughts and feelings without judgment. Regularly check in with each other to ensure understanding and address any communication gaps. Utilize conflict resolution skills to navigate differences and maintain connection.

Self-Care and Prioritization:

- Challenge: Neglecting self-care and failing to prioritize connection can lead to burnout and strained relationships.

- Strategy: Prioritize self-care and personal well-being to bring your best self to relationships. Allocate time for activities that recharge and rejuvenate you. Recognize that nurturing connections with loved ones is an integral part of self-care. Seek a balance between personal and relational needs, ensuring that both are adequately met.

By acknowledging these challenges and adopting strategies to address them, it is possible to maintain and deepen connections in the face of technology, busy lifestyles, and societal pressures. Proactive effort and deliberate choices can help preserve and nurture meaningful connections, leading to stronger, more fulfilling relationships.

CHAPTER 3: CONNECTION IN COMMUNITIES

THE IMPORTANCE OF CONNECTION IN BUILDING COMMUNITIES.

Connection plays a critical role in building strong and cohesive communities. It fosters a sense of belonging, trust, cooperation, and support among community members, leading to numerous benefits. Here are some key reasons why connection is vital for community strength:

Sense of Belonging and Inclusion: Connection creates a sense of belonging and inclusion within a community. When people feel connected to others, they develop a stronger attachment and commitment to the community. This sense of belonging enhances overall community cohesion, creating a supportive and welcoming environment for all individuals.

Social Support Networks: Connection enables the formation of social support networks within communities. These networks provide emotional support, practical assistance, and resources during challenging times. When community members feel connected, they are more likely to reach out and support one another, creating a safety net that fosters resilience and well-being.

Increased Collaboration and Cooperation: Connection encourages collaboration and cooperation within a community. When individuals feel connected, they are more inclined to work together, share resources, and pool their skills and knowledge for the greater good of the community. Collaboration strengthens community initiatives, promotes collective problem-solving, and enables the community to address challenges more effectively.

Promotes Positive Social Interactions: Connection promotes positive social interactions within a community, fostering a friendly and inclusive atmosphere. Community members who are connected are more likely to engage in respectful communication, empathy, and mutual support. This positive social environment enhances community engagement and participation, leading to a stronger and vibrant community fabric.

Better Resilience and Problem-Solving: Connected communities are more resilient and better equipped to address challenges. When individuals are connected, they can tap into a diverse range of perspectives, skills, and resources. This diversity strengthens problem-solving abilities and enables the community to adapt and thrive in the face of adversity.

Improved Quality of Life: Connection significantly improves the quality of life within a community. Connected communities offer a rich social support system, opportunities for meaningful engagement, and a sense of shared purpose. This enhances overall community well-being, happiness, and satisfaction.

In summary, connection is crucial for building strong and cohesive communities. It fosters a sense of belonging, creates social support networks, encourages collaboration, and promotes positive social interactions. Through connection, communities become more resilient, capable of addressing challenges, and provide an enriched quality of life for all their members. By prioritizing connection, communities can create an environment where individuals thrive, and collective well-being is nurtured.

HOW CONNECTION FOSTERS EMPATHY AND COOPERATION

Connection plays a key role in fostering empathy, cooperation, and social support networks within communities. Here's an exploration of how connection contributes to these important aspects:

Empathy: Connection helps foster empathy by creating a deep understanding of others' feelings and perspectives. When individuals feel connected, they are more likely to engage in active listening, perspective-taking, and showing genuine care for others. This emotional connection allows individuals to relate to and empathize with the experiences, challenges, and joys of others. Empathy strengthens interpersonal relationships, promotes compassion, and enhances overall community cohesion.

Cooperation: Connection encourages cooperation within communities by promoting a sense of shared goals and mutual support. When individuals feel connected, they are more willing to collaborate, share resources, and work towards common objectives. Connected individuals recognize that their actions impact others and strive for collective benefits rather than individual gains. Cooperation fosters a sense of unity and allows communities to tackle challenges collectively, resulting in more effective problem-solving and shared success.

Social Support Networks: Connection is essential for the formation of social support networks within communities. When individuals feel connected, they are more likely to offer and seek support from others when needed. These networks provide a safety net, offering emotional support, practical assistance, advice, and resources during times of difficulty. Social support networks within connected communities foster resilience, reduce isolation, and strengthen overall well-being.

Enhanced Communication: Connection facilitates open and effective communication within communities. When individuals feel connected, they are more motivated to engage in respectful and empathetic communication. Clear and empathetic communication is vital for building understanding, resolving conflicts, and finding common ground. These communication skills lay the foundation for building strong relationships, facilitating cooperation, and nurturing empathy within the community.

Shared Identity and Values: Connection establishes a shared sense of identity and values within communities. When individuals feel connected, they develop a collective identity that involves a sense of belonging and shared purpose. This shared identity strengthens bonds between community members, fosters cooperation, and encourages support for one another. Shared values guide behavior, promote inclusivity, and enable communities to work together towards common goals.

By fostering connection within communities, empathy, cooperation, and social support networks flourish. Connection strengthens interpersonal relationships, builds understanding, and allows communities to collectively navigate challenges with resilience and compassion. The resulting social support networks and collaborative spirit contribute to the overall well-being and cohesiveness of the community as a whole.

EXAMPLES OF COMMUNITIES THAT PRIORITIZE CONNECTION

There are several successful examples of communities that prioritize connection and have achieved positive outcomes. Here are a few notable examples:

Blue Zones: Blue Zones are regions around the world where people experience higher longevity and rates of well-being. These communities, such as Okinawa in Japan, Sardinia in Italy, and Nicoya Peninsula in Costa Rica, prioritize connection and social cohesion. They place a strong emphasis on family, friendship, and social networks, which contribute to their residents' longer and healthier lives.

L'Arche: L'Arche is an international federation of communities where people with intellectual disabilities and those without disabilities live together in a spirit of mutual relationships, belonging, and care. These communities prioritize connection and the inclusion of all members, fostering a sense of dignity, purpose, and deep relationships. The positive outcomes include increased well-being, personal growth, and a more compassionate society.

Quaker Communities: Quaker communities, also known as Religious Society of Friends, emphasize connection, equality, and collective decision-making. These communities prioritize listening, respectful dialogue, and communal worship. The emphasis on connection results in strong social networks, a sense of belonging, and collaborative decision-making that shapes these communities' positive outcomes.

Transition Towns: Transition Towns are grassroots community initiatives focused on building local resilience and sustainability. These communities prioritize connection, cooperation, and active citizen participation. By creating spaces for people to connect, share resources, and take collective action, Transition Towns achieve positive outcomes such as reduced environmental impact, increased community resilience, and enhanced well-being.

Cohousing Communities: Cohousing communities are intentional communities where residents actively participate in the design and management of their neighborhood. These communities prioritize connection, shared spaces, and cooperation. By fostering connection through common areas, collaborative decision-making, and shared responsibilities, cohousing communities achieve positive outcomes like increased social support, reduced isolation, and enhanced quality of life.

These successful examples emphasize the importance of connection in achieving positive outcomes within a community. Prioritizing connection leads to increased well-being, inclusive social networks, cooperation, resilience, and a deeper sense of belonging. These communities demonstrate that nurturing connection leads to thriving individuals, closer relationships, and the creation of vibrant and resilient communities.

CHAPTER 4: CONNECTION AND PERSONAL GROWTH

HOW CONNECTIONS WITH OTHERS CAN FACILITATE PERSONAL GROWTH

Connections with others can facilitate personal growth and self-discovery in several ways:

Exchanging Perspectives and Ideas: Connecting with others exposes us to a diverse range of perspectives, experiences, and knowledge. Engaging in meaningful conversations and sharing ideas with others can challenge our assumptions, broaden our horizons, and expand our understanding of the world. This exposure to different viewpoints nurtures personal growth by encouraging us to question, reflect, and evolve our own beliefs and values.

Emotional Support and Encouragement: Strong connections provide a supportive network that offers emotional guidance, encouragement, and motivation. When we connect with individuals who believe in our potential, we are more likely to step out of our comfort zones, pursue our passions, and take risks. The emotional support and encouragement we receive from these connections foster personal growth, resilience, and the confidence to explore new avenues.

Learning from Role Models and Mentors: Connecting with mentors and role models who have achieved what we aspire to can greatly facilitate personal growth. These individuals can offer guidance, share their experiences and wisdom, and inspire us to strive for our goals. By cultivating these connections, we gain valuable insights, learn from their mistakes, and develop the skills and knowledge necessary for our own personal development.

Receiving Constructive Feedback: Connections provide us with a trusted circle of individuals who can provide constructive feedback. These connections can offer valuable insights, identify blind spots, and help us recognize areas for improvement. By being open to feedback and utilizing these connections as sources of constructive criticism, we gain self-awareness, refine our skills, and grow both personally and professionally.

Challenging Comfort Zones: Genuine connections encourage us to step out of our comfort zones and embrace new opportunities. Through shared experiences and support, these connections push us to take on challenges, confront fears, and explore untapped potential. Stepping outside our comfort zones fosters personal growth, resilience, and a deeper understanding of ourselves and our capabilities.

Reflection and Self-Discovery: Connections with others can serve as mirrors that reflect who we are, our strengths, and areas for development. Engaging in deep and honest conversations, receiving feedback, and sharing vulnerabilities with trusted connections help us gain self-insight and foster self-discovery. Through these connections, we learn more about ourselves, our values, passions, and aspirations, leading to a stronger sense of personal identity and purpose.

In summary, connections with others play a vital role in facilitating personal growth and self-discovery. By engaging in meaningful relationships, learning from others, receiving support and feedback, and stepping outside our comfort zones, we evolve, gain self-awareness, and unlock our potential. These connections provide the support, guidance, and inspiration necessary for personal growth and the journey of self-discovery.

THE ROLE OF MENTORS, SUPPORTIVE NETWORKS, AND DIVERSE PERSPECTIVES

Mentors, supportive networks, and diverse perspectives all play crucial roles in expanding one's horizons and promoting personal growth. Here's an exploration of their individual contributions:

Mentors: Mentors provide guidance, support, and wisdom based on their own experiences and expertise. They play an instrumental role in expanding one's horizons by:

Sharing knowledge: Mentors offer valuable insights, expertise, and practical advice in areas where they have expertise. Their guidance helps individuals gain new skills, navigate challenges, and capitalize on opportunities.

Challenging limitations: Mentors can identify and challenge limitations that individuals may impose on themselves. They provide encouragement and push mentees to step outside their comfort zones, explore new possibilities, and set higher goals.

Providing perspective: Mentors offer a broader perspective and can shed light on different pathways, career choices, and personal development opportunities. They encourage mentees to consider options they may not have otherwise explored.

Supportive Networks: Supportive networks, such as

friends, colleagues, and like-minded individuals, foster personal growth by:

Providing emotional support: Supportive networks offer a sense of belonging and emotional support during setbacks, challenges, and successes. They provide a safe space to share vulnerabilities, seek advice, and gain encouragement, which boosts resilience and personal growth.

Sharing resources: Networks provide access to diverse resources, including information, opportunities, and connections. Through supportive networks, individuals can tap into a wealth of knowledge and experiences, expanding their horizons and accessing new possibilities.

Offering different perspectives: Supportive networks consist of individuals with a variety of backgrounds, experiences, and perspectives. Engaging with this diversity exposes individuals to different ways of thinking, challenging existing beliefs, and expanding one's understanding of the world.

Diverse Perspectives: Engaging with diverse perspectives expands one's horizons by:

Encouraging empathy and understanding: Exposure to diverse perspectives cultivates empathy and understanding towards individuals from different backgrounds, cultures, and experiences. It broadens our capacity to embrace different viewpoints, challenge biases, and break down stereotypes.

Fostering creativity and innovation: Diverse perspectives spark creativity as they offer new angles, insights, and problem-solving approaches. When we engage with ideas and perspectives different from our own, we gain a broader scope for innovative thinking and foster personal growth through creative exploration.

Challenging assumptions and biases: Diverse perspectives challenge our own beliefs and assumptions, forcing us to critically examine our viewpoints. This process helps break down biases, fosters intellectual growth, and promotes open-mindedness.

In summary, mentors, supportive networks, and diverse perspectives are instrumental in expanding one's horizons and promoting personal growth. Mentors offer guidance and wisdom, supportive networks provide emotional support and shared resources, and diverse perspectives challenge assumptions and foster empathy. By embracing these influences, individuals gain new insights, expand their understanding of the world, and unlock their own potential for personal and intellectual growth.

THE TRANSFORMATIVE POWER OF CONNECTION

The transformative power of connection can be a key factor in overcoming challenges and achieving goals. Here's an exploration of how connection can bring about transformation in such situations:

Emotional Support and Resilience: Connection provides emotional support during challenging times, helping individuals build resilience and navigate obstacles. When facing challenges, having a supportive network of individuals who believe in our abilities and offer encouragement can make all the difference. Connection fosters a sense of reassurance, motivation, and optimism, empowering individuals to persevere through hardships and stay focused on their goals.

Collaboration and Synergy: Connection facilitates collaboration and fosters the power of collective effort. By connecting with others who share similar goals or complementary skills and expertise, individuals can pool their resources, knowledge, and perspectives. Collaborative connections enable the sharing of ideas, brainstorming, and problem-solving, leading to innovative solutions and a greater chance of achieving goals.

Networks and Opportunities: Connection expands individuals' access to networks and opens doors to new opportunities. By connecting with people who have relevant connections or insights, individuals can tap into a wider range of resources, such as information, mentorship, or potential collaborations. These connections can provide guidance, advice, and connections that accelerate progress towards goals.

Accountability and Motivation: Connection helps foster accountability and motivation in the pursuit of goals. Sharing goals with supportive connections creates a sense of responsibility and encourages individuals to stay committed. Furthermore, these connections can serve as sources of motivation, providing regular encouragement, and celebrating milestones, which enhances one's perseverance and determination.

Mentorship and Guidance: Connection with mentors or experienced individuals provides invaluable guidance and advice on how to navigate challenges and achieve goals. Mentors offer insights based on their own experiences, helping individuals avoid potential pitfalls, make informed decisions, and learn from their mentor's wisdom. This mentorship connection can foster personal growth, increase self-confidence, and provide a roadmap for success.

Learning and Growth: Connection provides opportunities for learning and personal growth. Through connections with individuals who possess different skills, knowledge, and experiences, individuals can broaden their perspectives, acquire new insights, and develop new skills. This continuous learning and growth facilitate adaptation and improvement, empowering individuals to overcome challenges and thrive while pursuing their goals.

In summary, connection has a transformative power when it comes to overcoming challenges and achieving goals. It provides emotional support, encourages collaboration, expands networks, fosters accountability, and promotes personal growth. By embracing the power of connection, individuals can navigate obstacles, seize opportunities, and realize their full potential while transforming their lives.

CHAPTER 5: CONNECTION AND SOCIETAL PROGRESS

HOW CONNECTION CAN DRIVE SOCIETAL PROGRESS AND INNOVATION.

Connection plays a pivotal role in driving societal progress and fostering innovation. Here's an analysis of how connection contributes to these areas:

Collaboration and Knowledge Sharing: Connection stimulates collaboration and the sharing of knowledge and ideas. When individuals and groups connect, they bring together diverse perspectives, experiences, and expertise. By sharing their knowledge, insights, and skills, they can collaborate on finding innovative solutions to societal challenges. These collaborative efforts lead to new discoveries, advancements, and solutions that drive societal progress and foster innovation.

Cross-Pollination of Ideas: Connection facilitates the cross-pollination of ideas across different disciplines and industries. When individuals from various backgrounds and domains come together, they exchange ideas and perspectives that can spark creativity and innovation. Breaking down silos and connecting different areas of expertise facilitates the transfer of knowledge and expertise, enabling fresh approaches and breakthroughs within society.

Access to Resources and Support: Connection provides access to resources, networks, and support systems that are crucial for societal progress and innovation.

Connected individuals can tap into a wide range of resources, such as funding, infrastructure, research data, and mentorship. These resources fuel innovation, allowing individuals and groups to develop and implement ideas that have a positive impact on society.

Collective Impact and Scale: Connection allows for a collective impact and scale of innovation. When individuals and groups connect, they can pool their resources, expertise, and efforts to tackle complex societal problems. Connected networks can amplify the impact of individual innovations and initiatives by spreading knowledge and best practices, leading to widespread positive change.

Diversity and Inclusive Innovation: Connection enables diversity and inclusive innovation. By connecting with individuals from different backgrounds, cultures, and perspectives, innovation becomes more inclusive, reflecting the needs and experiences of a broader range of society. This diversity fosters problem-solving approaches that are more comprehensive, effective, and relevant to the communities they aim to serve.

Feedback and Iteration: Connection facilitates feedback and iteration in the innovation process. Through connection with customers, end-users, and stakeholders, innovators can gather valuable insights, refine their ideas, and iterate on their solutions. This continuous feedback loop ensures that innovations address real-world needs and evolve in response to changing societal demands, driving progress and improvement.

In summary, connection drives societal progress and innovation by fostering collaboration, cross-pollination of ideas, access to resources, collective impact, diversity, and feedback. By establishing and nurturing connections, individuals and groups can leverage their collective knowledge, skills, and resources to address societal challenges, drive innovation, and create positive change that benefits society as a whole.

THE IMPORTANCE OF COLLABORATION

Collaboration, cross-cultural understanding, and inclusive dialogue are of utmost importance in addressing global challenges. Here's an exploration of their significance:

Collaboration: Global challenges, such as climate change, poverty, and political conflicts, are complex and interconnected. Collaboration brings together diverse stakeholders, including individuals, organizations, communities, and nations, to collectively work towards solutions. By collaborating, resources can be pooled, expertise can be shared, and efforts can be coordinated, leading to more effective and sustainable outcomes.

Cross-Cultural Understanding: Global challenges often stem from cultural differences, disparities, and misunderstandings. Cross-cultural understanding promotes empathy, tolerance, and appreciation for different perspectives, beliefs, and traditions. By seeking to understand the complexities of diverse cultures and backgrounds, we can move beyond stereotypes and biases, fostering cooperation, mutual respect, and collaborative problem-solving.

Inclusive Dialogue: Inclusive dialogue involves actively engaging individuals and groups from different backgrounds, identities, and marginalized communities. By creating platforms for inclusive dialogue, the voices of marginalized populations can be heard, and their experiences and perspectives can inform solutions to global challenges. Inclusive dialogue ensures that decision-making processes are equitable and representative, leading to more effective and sustainable outcomes that address the needs of all individuals.

Collective Wisdom and Innovation: Collaboration, cross-cultural understanding, and inclusive dialogue harness collective wisdom and promote innovation. In diverse and inclusive environments, ideas from different perspectives are brought forward, stimulating creative thinking and innovative problem-solving approaches. By leveraging the diversity of knowledge, experiences, and perspectives, new solutions to global challenges can emerge that consider multiple dimensions and complexities.

Building Trust and Partnerships: Collaboration, cross-cultural understanding, and inclusive dialogue foster trust and build partnerships between individuals, communities, and nations. Establishing trust is crucial for effective collaboration, as it allows diverse stakeholders to work together towards shared goals. Mutual respect, open communication, and valuing different contributions strengthen both local and global partnerships, enhancing the potential for collective action and common solutions.

Sustainable Development and Peace: Addressing global challenges requires sustainable development and peaceful coexistence. Collaboration, cross-cultural understanding, and inclusive dialogue are intrinsic to fostering sustainable development, as they ensure that solutions are inclusive, equitable, and address the needs of present and future generations. Additionally, these practices contribute to peacebuilding, as dialogue and understanding facilitate the resolution of conflicts, reduce tensions, and promote peaceful relationships between different countries and communities.

In summary, collaboration, cross-cultural understanding, and inclusive dialogue are vital in addressing global challenges. They promote collective action, foster empathy and understanding, harness the power of diverse perspectives, build partnerships, and contribute to sustainable development and peace. By embracing these principles, we can work together to tackle complex global problems and create a more inclusive, equitable, and harmonious world.

EXAMPLES OF SUCCESSFUL COLLABORATIONS

There are several notable examples of successful collaborations that have made a positive impact. Here are a few:

The Paris Agreement: The Paris Agreement is an international collaboration that aims to combat climate change. Signed by nearly every country in the world, this agreement sets targets for reducing greenhouse gas emissions, adapting to the impacts of climate change, and providing financial support to developing nations. The collaboration between countries has led to increased global momentum, awareness, and action towards mitigating climate change and preserving the planet for future generations.

The Human Genome Project: The Human Genome Project was an international scientific collaboration that aimed to map the entire human genome. This groundbreaking project involved scientists and researchers from many countries, sharing data, resources, and knowledge. The collaboration significantly accelerated progress, resulting in the completion of the genome sequence ahead of schedule. The project has led to immense advancements in understanding genetics, personalized medicine, and disease prevention, revolutionizing the field of genomics.

The Apollo Moon Missions: The Apollo Moon Missions were a series of spacecraft missions led by NASA in collaboration with various international partners. These missions involved nations pooling their scientific, technical, and financial resources to achieve the common goal of landing humans on the moon. The successful collaborations not only led to profound scientific discoveries but also inspired generations and showcased the potential of global cooperation and exploration.

The Global Polio Eradication Initiative: The Global Polio Eradication Initiative is a collaboration between governments, organizations like WHO and UNICEF, and several partnering organizations. By pooling resources, expertise, and strategies, this initiative has made extraordinary progress towards eradicating polio globally. Through vaccination campaigns, surveillance systems, and community engagement, the initiative has prevented millions of cases and brought the world closer to the goal of eradication.

The Open Source Movement: The Open Source movement is a collaborative approach to software development that encourages the sharing of source code and collaborative innovation. This movement has led to the creation of numerous successful projects, such as the Linux operating system and the Apache web server. The collaborative model allows for rapid development, peer review, and community-driven improvements, resulting in highly reliable and innovative software solutions.

These examples highlight the positive impact of collaborations. They demonstrate that when multiple stakeholders come together, combining their resources, expertise, and efforts, remarkable progress can be made towards solving complex challenges and achieving common goals. Such collaborations serve as inspirational models for addressing global issues through cooperation, innovation, and collective action.

CHAPTER 6: CONNECTION FOR GLOBAL UNITY

THE URGENT NEED FOR CONNECTION TODAY

In today's polarized world, the urgent need for connection is more crucial than ever. Here are a few reasons why connection is essential in addressing polarization:

Bridging Divides: Connection plays a vital role in bridging divides between different groups and individuals. In a polarized world, people tend to retreat into echo chambers and surround themselves with like-minded perspectives, perpetuating divisions. Connection breaks down barriers by fostering understanding, empathy, and dialogue across ideological, cultural, and socio-economic lines. It allows individuals to find common ground, build trust, and work towards shared goals.

Encouraging Empathy: Connection cultivates empathy, the ability to understand and relate to the experiences and feelings of others. In a polarized world, people often struggle to understand and empathize with those who hold different viewpoints or come from diverse backgrounds. Connection fosters empathy by bringing people together, encouraging active listening, and promoting genuine curiosity about others' experiences. This empathy humanizes "the other," breaking down stereotypes, prejudices, and biases.

Promoting Constructive Dialogue: Connection fosters an environment conducive to constructive dialogue, where diverse perspectives can be heard and engaged with respect and open-mindedness. In a polarized world, conversations often devolve into shouting matches or binary thinking. Connection encourages active listening, mutual respect, and the willingness to consider different viewpoints. It allows for nuanced discussions, constructive disagreements, and the exploration of shared values and common ground.

Building Stronger Communities: Connection strengthens communities by promoting social cohesion, cooperation, and resilience. In a polarized world, communities often face divisions that hinder progress and social well-being. Connection brings individuals together, fostering a sense of belonging, shared purpose, and collective identity. It encourages collaboration, solutions-oriented thinking, and the ability to address challenges collectively. Stronger communities built on connection can overcome polarization and work towards inclusive and thriving societies.

Encouraging Active Citizenship: Connection fuels active citizenship, motivating individuals to engage in their communities and contribute to positive change. In a polarized world, apathy and disengagement can prevail due to a sense of hopelessness or the belief that individual actions have no impact. Connection reminds people of their interconnectedness and the power they possess to effect change. It inspires civic participation, volunteerism, and collective action towards common goals, driving transformational efforts.

In summary, connection is urgently needed in today's polarized world to bridge divides, encourage empathy, promote constructive dialogue, build stronger communities, and nurture active citizenship. By promoting connection, we can work towards a more inclusive, tolerant, and unified global community that can address the complex challenges we face with empathy, understanding, and collaborative solutions.

THE POTENTIAL TO BRIDGE DIVIDES

Connection has significant potential to bridge divides and foster mutual understanding among individuals and nations in several ways:

Creating Common Ground: Connection can create common ground by emphasizing shared values, aspirations, or goals. By focusing on our shared humanity, connection helps individuals recognize similarities, rather than solely focusing on differences. Finding areas of commonality fosters understanding, breaks down barriers, and encourages collaborative problem-solving.

Encouraging Empathy and Perspective-Taking: Connection cultivates empathy and the ability to see things from others' perspectives. When individuals connect with one another, they are more likely to listen, understand, and empathize with different backgrounds, experiences, and viewpoints. This empathetic understanding builds bridges and fosters mutual respect and compassion.

Facilitating Dialogue and Communication: Connection promotes open and constructive dialogue among individuals and nations. By creating spaces for honest and respectful communication, individuals can engage in substantive discussions, bridge cultural or ideological gaps, and work towards mutual understanding. Connection enables meaningful exchange, helping to break down stereotypes, challenge biases, and debunk misconceptions.

Encouraging Cultural Exchange and Interactions: Connection encourages cultural exchange and interactions, enabling individuals to learn about different cultures, traditions, and ways of life. Through cultural exchange programs, travel, or even virtual connections, individuals can build relationships and gain firsthand exposure to other perspectives. These interactions foster appreciation for diversity, increase cultural competence, and nurture understanding.

Promoting Collaboration and Cooperation: Connection facilitates collaboration and cooperation among individuals and nations, emphasizing the shared pursuit of common goals. By connecting and working together, individuals can recognize that collective efforts often yield greater outcomes than individual endeavors. This realization encourages a shift from an "us vs. them" mentality to a collaborative mindset, fostering understanding and joint problem-solving.

Highlighting Interdependence and Global Challenges: Connection helps individuals recognize their interdependence and the interconnectedness of global challenges. By connecting with individuals from different countries and cultures, individuals can understand that global issues, such as climate change, poverty, or pandemics, require collective action and cooperation to find effective solutions. Connection reinforces the notion that individuals and nations are part of a larger global community, instilling a sense of responsibility towards each other's well-being.

In summary, connection has the potential to bridge divides and foster mutual understanding among individuals and nations. By emphasizing common ground, enhancing empathy, promoting respectful dialogue, encouraging cultural exchange, fostering collaboration, and highlighting interdependence, connection serves as a powerful catalyst for building understanding, empathy, and unity in an increasingly interconnected world.

WAYS TO PROMOTE CONNECTION ON A GLOBAL SCALE

Promoting connection on a global scale requires various approaches that foster cultural exchange, diplomacy, and international cooperation. Here are some ways to promote connection globally:

Cultural Exchanges: Cultural exchanges facilitate mutual understanding and connection by encouraging the exchange of ideas, traditions, and perspectives. Programs that enable people from different countries to live, study, or work in another culture enhance cross-cultural understanding. This can include student exchange programs, artist residencies, international volunteer opportunities, and hosting cultural festivals that celebrate diverse traditions.

Diplomacy and Dialogue: Diplomacy and dialogue play a crucial role in promoting connection and resolving conflicts on a global scale. Engaging in diplomatic efforts, such as peace negotiations and dialogue initiatives, can help build trust, bridge divides, and find common ground. Multilateral forums, such as the United Nations, provide platforms for open dialogue and diplomacy among nations, fostering connections and fostering cooperation.

International Cooperation: International cooperation encourages collaboration among countries to address global challenges and achieve common goals. Through partnerships, joint projects, and resource-sharing, countries can work together to tackle issues like climate change, public health crises, poverty eradication, and more. Global initiatives and organizations, such as the World Health Organization, international development agencies, and multinational corporations, facilitate international cooperation, connecting countries and promoting collaboration.

Technology and Digital Connectivity: Technology and digital connectivity offer means for promoting connection on a global scale. Platforms like social media, video conferencing, and digital communities have the potential to connect individuals across geographical boundaries, providing opportunities for dialogue and collaboration. Leveraging technology for virtual conferences, webinars, and knowledge-sharing platforms enables people from diverse backgrounds to connect and exchange ideas without physical barriers.

Educational Programs and Partnerships: Educational programs and partnerships foster connections and cross-cultural understanding among students, educators, and institutions. Initiatives like exchange programs, joint research projects, and distance learning opportunities bring together people from different countries and backgrounds. These educational collaborations cultivate meaningful connections, promote cultural exchange, and contribute to global perspectives among future leaders and professionals.

International Sports and Cultural Events: International sports and cultural events, such as the Olympic Games, World Cups, and arts festivals, provide platforms for people worldwide to come together and celebrate cultural diversity. These events foster positive interactions, appreciation for different cultures, and a sense of unity and connection through shared experiences.

In summary, promoting connection on a global scale requires efforts through cultural exchanges, diplomacy, international cooperation, technology, education, and engaging platforms like sports and cultural events. These approaches enable greater understanding, bridge divides, and foster unity among diverse individuals and nations, contributing to a more globally connected and collaborative world.

CONCLUSION:

RECAP

In summary, here are the main arguments for why the world needs connection:

Human Need: Connection is a fundamental human need rooted in our biology and psychology. It contributes to our well-being, sense of belonging, and emotional fulfillment.

Meaningful Relationships: Connection fosters meaningful relationships that provide emotional support, intimacy, and personal growth. It strengthens bonds, enhances communication, and promotes overall relationship satisfaction.

Community Cohesion: Connection builds strong and cohesive communities by fostering empathy, cooperation, social support networks, and shared values. It enables communities to address challenges collectively, promote social well-being, and thrive.

Personal Growth and Self-Discovery: Connection facilitates personal growth and self-discovery by exposing individuals to diverse perspectives, fostering empathy, providing mentorship, and promoting collaboration. It expands horizons, challenges assumptions, and facilitates personal development.

Societal Progress and Innovation: Connection drives societal progress through collaboration, cross-cultural understanding, inclusive dialogue, and the collective expertise and resources that connection brings. It stimulates innovation, solves global challenges, and promotes a more inclusive and equitable society.

Global Unity: Connection promotes global unity by bridging divides, fostering mutual understanding, and encouraging cooperation among individuals and nations. It highlights our interconnectedness, mutual responsibilities, and the need for collective action to address global challenges.

Ultimately, the world needs connection because it is essential for our well-being, personal growth, community cohesion, societal progress, and global unity. Connection fosters empathy, cooperation, and understanding, and it enables us to address challenges, achieve collective goals, and build a more compassionate, inclusive, and interconnected world.

THE ROLE OF INDIVIDUALS IN FOSTERING CONNECTION

The role of individuals is pivotal in fostering connection and creating a more interconnected world. Here's why individuals play a crucial part:

Building Relationships: Individuals have the power to initiate and nurture meaningful relationships. By taking the initiative to connect with others, showing genuine interest, and cultivating deep connections, individuals lay the foundation for a more connected world. It starts with simple acts of kindness, empathy, and reaching out to forge bonds of understanding and companionship.

Demonstrating Empathy: Individuals can actively practice empathy, putting themselves in others' shoes and understanding their perspectives and experiences. By approaching interactions with empathy, individuals can bridge divides, dissolve biases, and foster understanding and compassion. Small acts of empathy have a ripple effect, creating a more inclusive and interconnected world.

Creating Inclusive Spaces: Individuals can create inclusive spaces where diverse voices, backgrounds, and perspectives are valued and respected. By promoting inclusivity and actively seeking out diverse opinions, individuals can create environments that encourage connection, dialogue, and collaboration. Inclusive spaces foster a sense of belonging and make room for a variety of experiences and ideas.

Practicing Active Listening: Active listening is a powerful skill that cultivates connection. Individuals can hone their ability to listen attentively, without judgment or interruption. By truly hearing and understanding others, individuals can foster deeper connections, build trust, and create an atmosphere of openness and respect.

Promoting Collaboration: Individuals can champion collaboration and cooperation in their personal and professional lives. By seeking opportunities to work together, leveraging collective strengths, and breaking down silos, individuals promote collaboration on a wider scale. Collaboration brings diverse perspectives and expertise to the table, fostering innovative solutions and achieving shared goals.

Spreading Positivity and Kindness: Individuals can have a profound impact through acts of positivity and kindness. Simple gestures like offering support, showing appreciation, or lending a helping hand can create a ripple effect of connection and inspire others to do the same. By fostering a culture of kindness and positivity, individuals contribute to a more interconnected and compassionate world.

In conclusion, individuals hold immense power and responsibility in fostering connection and creating a more interconnected world. By building relationships, practicing empathy, creating inclusive spaces, practicing active listening, promoting collaboration, and spreading positivity, individuals can make a significant difference. It starts with each individual recognizing their capacity to influence and actively choosing to prioritize connection in their interactions, relationships, and daily lives. Together, individuals can shape a more connected, empathetic, and united world for the benefit of all.

LASTLY

In a world that often feels disconnected, prioritizing connection is not only crucial but also holds the power to transform not just our personal lives but society as a whole. Here's some inspiration to prioritize connection and work towards building a more empathetic and united society:

Embrace the Power of Connection: Connection has the remarkable ability to heal, inspire, and uplift. By prioritizing meaningful connections in our personal lives, we can experience a profound sense of belonging, support, and joy. Recognize that every interaction, no matter how small, has the potential to make a positive impact on someone else's life.

Practice Empathy and Understanding: Cultivate a deep sense of empathy towards others, striving to understand their experiences, perspectives, and emotions. By stepping into someone else's shoes, we build bridges of understanding and foster an environment of compassion, kindness, and unity.

Nurture Relationships: Prioritize the relationships that matter most to you. Invest time and effort in cultivating meaningful connections with family, friends, and communities. Engage in open and honest conversations, actively listen, and be present. This investment in relationships fosters trust and resilience, strengthening the fabric of our society.

Create Inclusive Spaces: Actively work towards creating inclusive spaces where diversity is celebrated and respected. Encourage open dialogue, seek out different perspectives, and create an environment that values and welcomes voices from all backgrounds. By fostering inclusivity, we foster connection and build a society where everyone feels heard and valued.

Seek Common Grounds: Look for commonalities rather than focusing solely on differences. Find shared goals, values, or passions that can bring people together. By emphasizing the things that unite us, we create opportunities for collaboration and growth, contributing to a more united and harmonious society.

Lead by Example: Be a beacon of connection and empathy in your actions and interactions. Inspire others to prioritize connection by practicing active listening, offering support, and demonstrating acts of kindness. By leading with empathy, you create a ripple effect that can inspire positive change in others and contribute to a more connected and compassionate society.

Remember, connection starts with each one of us. By prioritizing connection in our personal lives and working towards a more empathetic and united society, we can create a ripple effect of positive change that extends far beyond ourselves. Let us embark on this journey together, with open hearts and open minds, as we build a world where connection and empathy thrive.

connection and empathy thrive.